T0012494

CELEBRATE PRIDE
WITH LOCKHEED MARTIN

ALSO BY JAKE BYRNE

The Tide

CELEBRATE PRIDE WITH LOCKHEED MARTIN

JAKE BYRNE

POEMS

A Buckrider Book

Published by Buckrider Books,
an imprint of Wolsak and Wynn Publishers
280 James Street North
Hamilton, ON L8R2L3
www.wolsakandwynn.ca

Editor for Buckrider Books: Paul Vermeersch
Editor: Liz Howard | Copy editor: Ashley Hisson
Cover and interior design: Kilby Smith-McGregor
Author photograph: Jessica Laforet
Typeset in DM Sans, Urgent Telegram AOE, and Adobe Caslon Pro
Printed by Coach House Printing Company, Toronto, Canada

10 9 8 7 6 5 4 3 2 1

 Canada Council Conseil des Arts
for the Arts du Canada  Canadä

The publisher gratefully acknowledges the support of the Ontario Arts Council, the Canada Council for the Arts and the Government of Canada.

Library and Archives Canada Cataloguing in Publication

Title: Celebrate pride with Lockheed Martin / Jake Byrne.
Names: Byrne, Jake (Poet), author.
Description: Poems.
Identifiers: Canadiana 20230181619 | ISBN 9781989496640 (softcover)
Classification: LCC PS8603.Y75 C45 2023 | DDC C811/.6—dc23

The color of money is
Night-vision green.

Ben Lerner, "Mean Free Path," *Mean Free Path*

The countless generations rise from underground this afternoon
And fall like rain.
I never thought that I would live to see the towers fall again.

Frederick Seidel, "The Bush Administration," *Ooga-Booga*

DISPATCHES: CELEBRATE PRIDE WITH LOCKHEED MARTIN

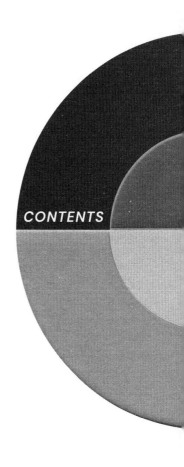

CONTENTS

A BOUQUET OF
KETCHUP–FLAVOURED ROSES

It is sixteen Celsius in February

I am screaming

Borders close

Munitions transport

Projections evaporate

Supernovae

Oak outside my window

Buds so early it won't flower

Not great for anyone who enjoys

Being alive

Here's a hundred

Take me anywhere

Just drive

Knowledge works in secret places

And its works are sprouting thorns

My boyfriend texts me

Now that Jessica's taken over the accounts

Now that Jessica's doing his job or whatever

He is allowed to die

I try to sleep but I can't

My boyfriend texts me to clarify

He doesn't want to kill himself

Just wants to go for a hike along the lakeshore

Until he turns into sun-dappled fog

Until he isn't anymore

And while it's true

That all cold people will look you dead

In eye and mutter

Actually, it's that I care too much

But it is

I do

It is not his fault

He was conceived in winter

His blood, gelid

Has just begun

To warmly flow in

February sun

See I never needed

The actual bomb

The bomb was an idea

We deserved what was coming

And because the idea

Prefigured the bomb

The idea of the bomb and the work of the bomb are one.

I want spring

To bust open on me like fistfuls of girls

In yellow dresses

Girls

Drooling hot blood

From full lips

A bouquet of ketchup-flavoured roses made of Doritos

Wish I made that up

Earthlings

You are caught in

A vast and inscrutable system

Beyond your control

My feeling

The world

Doesn't have fifty more good years in it

Maybe not even five

I've perversely

Transmuted into

Tasteless nude selfies

Follicle transplants

Deadlifts

I need you to know

That I know

But also

I've never looked hotter

Not so hot as

Six times the surface temperature

Of the sun

Mind you

The sun is a fact

Of the world that I live in

As is the bomb

And the fact of a mountain

Beautiful as the curve

Of my seatmate's ass in white Calvins

Peeking out the scoop of his jeans

On this train I ride to get to work

Maybe somebody would want to read that

If any readers are alive

Forehead on cold train window

My father's paranoia snakes into my

Poems

Like a licking tendril of flame it pursues me

Through dreams he carries an axe and a grin

My father who is ill and yet is not ill

Just as I am ill and yet am not ill

Living in a world that is ill too

Not how I'd like it to be

Swish I am prone

Slurping mauve into linen

He comes bearing razor blades as a gift

I ask myself

Is anybody really sick

Like my boyfriend

Or Dad

Or does the world's illness express itself through us

But then my boyfriend casually texts

He doesn't want to die

Just wants to go to sleep and not wake up

And I remember that

Yes

People in this world have been sickened

Infected with prototypes and schematics

Fevered with ideas

That boil into gases

That propel metal into

Soft and mutable bodies

                              I love you. Please stay alive

See modernity is only

A feeling

Nothing good could come from this

See I never needed

The actual bomb

Balloons are Nature's flowers

Apotheosis

Kia Sorento

Plastics concatenate

Packages fulgurate

Ashtrays coruscate

Neonicotinoids dazzle

Methane clathrates

Livers fulminate

There's an abscess in the throat of this world

A boon that begs for a balm

I was having

Too much fun

Panic grass and feverfew

I was just trying to live in the world   Wasn't I?

I was just trying to live

DISPATCHES:

CELEBRATE PRIDE WITH LOCKHEED MARTIN

DISASTER TOURISM I

At twenty-one having quit both job
And school in order to pursue
Taking ecstasy full-time, I borrowed
Ten thousand Canadian dollars from my father
To drink and tour some death camps

My father I have since repaid

DISASTER TOURISM II

The sun went down over the guard tower
I'm not sure I can describe the colour to you
Though that is the chief responsibility of the
Job I am "just doing," and having now borne witness to
The collected hair, broken spectacles
Empty shoes of millions dead
And even worse than that: a lumpenprole
English tourist and her son behaving rudely
As our guide motioned us to
The brick wall beyond the ovens.
Our tour concluded and I found the bathrooms shut
And resolving I would not
Whip "it" out and piss on Auschwitz
I spent the ninety-minute bus trip back to Kraków
Alone in total darkness, straining
Bargaining to a God I did not then believe in
To keep my bladder's walls from breaching
Never again. It will never happen again.
Not on my watch   Just
Ten kilometres remain

DISASTER TOURISM III

I was not prepared for how
Beautiful the *Arbeit Macht Frei* gate would look
With the sun behind it, and a late-afternoon October fog
Lazily and playfully roving round the grounds
One thinks that no grass or flowers should grow there in sympathy
In perpetuity. Wrapped in orange-gold October ivy
In my memory

I came prepared for death, solemnity
I had not steeled myself for beauty
I returned to the hostel at which I was the only guest
And since those were the years
I dreamed of writing nightly
While writing nothing
But my name on debit statements at the bar
Encased myself on cocktails called *beton* or
"Concrete" – took notes for a novel I would never write
'Til I had drunk enough to pass out again

alone

INTIMACY

Please
      Pull the spinels growing from my eyes. I cannot see

Every day feels like
I cannot grasp life among persons
Whose language I grew up speaking a pidgin of
Whose mysteries were truncated for my consumption
Who laugh as I emulate their proud and curious fashions

      Love is the communion you so desperately cleave to
      Wanting it to melt on your tongue and become part of you
      Open a door and gently push you into the wide room
      Where everyone you've ever loved is there clapping for you
      There are squealing balloons

That is where I want to live. Not here among
Charming men
With moonlit agendas
Men who kill and plunder and
Laugh
As clowns do
Painted in the swollen dark

      In the sunny piazza I held my greasy hair in my hands

1-900-CUM-FIEND

I'm too horny to wear my human suit today
Need Antoine's boyfriend to wield a flaming sword inside me
On this plane, there are no absolutes.
Antoine has anodized the air above the pass.
To drink the piss of a man when he demands
Why, it's only the most natural thing in the world
And spoken from a mouth so curved I now agree

What river through time are you swimming down!
Why does the sperm cling to your hair like that!
As life does!

In the manila-enveloped quiet of the library
Cold roses on wet concrete, salty-sweet risks
A lateral move over to rusted cooling towers. Grain elevators

Wait for our offerings. Miasma venting squirrel carcasses
Caught in breakers' teeth. Here the altars of Winter
His remote and inaccessible palaces where
Video lottery terminals breathe me in

On video you can watch an axon squirm
In a way you can see thought
Watch the lonely pas de deux of the eighteen-wheeler
Greasy white flanks stitched up with duct tape
The honeycomb tarry and black with spoiled seasons
I'm not fucking around. I want you to say

Thank you. Say thank you to the heralds
Of Spring, the Great Deceiver
How can I be open and honest here
In my life as I look up from this page?
Chase me into the costly darkness
Of this unlovable bar for I am   lonely.
                                        Are you   lonely too?

                        Does my body make you feel lonely?
Maybe with some practice   my body could become my body too
I want communion under my tongue
A word that unlocks bodies like doors
            All these stacks of greedy kindling inside me
            Crying for a bonny match …

ADVENTURE TIME II

We passed on horseback without speaking
  Through cities of bleached bone and powdered glass
  When I plunged my pen into the lich's mirror
You told me you'd given me everything I needed

My marital bed a ditch where milk-sky and memory admix
  You said true love never promises to stay
  Some needs come second to the resumé
Relapse with me. Let's be adepts playing at cantrips

A pocketful of perfumed air
  Chokecherries' dark epistles
  Your cum congealing on the hair of my chest
These magic missiles

But all illusions wane, crumble like lichen in a dry season
  I can recall the rite but cannot perform the ritual
  You can lead a hearse to water, but it's no Viking funeral
Not for the cursèd opaque waterbed of your elfin immigration lawyer

Not for the scarred arms of the berserker otter
  Who fucked me raw against the wall
  Promising all the while he'd pull out graceful as
A siege of herons from the water

He showed me how to rip a bezoar from the stomach of a kid
  A sea of mead could not satisfy my id
  Nor could a kiss land gentle as a fist
My harvest-sworn companion, how did we come to this?

I meant to say I loved you
For you I'd remake the world as mine
Who cares. It doesn't matter. Forget about it. Nevermind

TAKE ME TO CHURCH

Anoint me in green juice and semen
I want to join the Fellowship of Now.
I need to find myself a rock
to weigh my pockets to the bottom of the creek.
The Earth waits to take us all back into it
as it lets out one final explosive sigh. All of us
gathered here at desks and wheels and café tables,
holding a shared hallucination we call work.
    The work will never hold us back.
So hold me now. I need to feel
that everything will be okay
that the oceans will cool
the money will never, ever run out.
That we'll be given life without strictures and breath within reason.
In the race all runners run, but only one can win the prize.
So I've swallowed my portion of filth
I have danced in my dressings of sin
I will cling to this

BALLOONFEST '86

World record for simultaneous release of balloons. Two dead.

O Cleveland, the spectacle!
    Concerned meteorologists agree: when a balloon pops
the helium, three hundred times its weight

    in gold, rockets out to space. What
        hollow value do you assign a death rattle?
    The suit was settled

    out of court, in camera. The world
        is always wanting
    a widow, a quiet little plot to lay lilies.

    Remember, drowning Ithacan sailor
        that charity faileth not but kisses
    the sky like a child's belief.

Are these rainbow sprinkles in your vision
    or an unfathomable reel
of two million balloons?

Only comfort cold as Erie to be had.
Latex, masquerading as lily pad.

RAEKUURO

In my dream, I flew low –
white-knuckled controls,
case of the shakes, pilot's licence
an empty signifier in my pocket –
over a country so flat
I could see the map overlaid on the territory.
Wattling crags. Lappish farmhouses,
jays' eggs, speckled with sleet.
Pines that shook off snow in the wind
like Samoyeds. My mother, there in
the co-pilot's chair, asleep,
hunks of amber on her eyelids.
It went on like this –
the countryside, my dream, my life –
'til something wicked up from the Baltic
green where the sea tongues the port
and blew my mother's scarf into my face.

I lose control. The plane groans
groundward, toward the country manor
of my father's father's wartime enemy.
To have thought my fate was a vehicle I'd steer
that my destiny hadn't been determined for me long ago
that the dream would not end in fire
moving outwards from the point of impact –

In the realm of the waking, at the port,
Piia whispers over salty licorice
that the surrounding houses are all the same material,
same height, having been bombed in '44.

Maybe it wouldn't be so hard after all to rebuild somewhere new.
But this is the petty luxury of the tourist.
Snails wink at me from a twenty-euro pizza, and
my face precipitates, because someone has given me
kindness the texture of cloudberry jam.
Maybe I'll marry a woman
whose name means *wind* in the local language.
But here comes a mistral with its own agenda.
Hail pelts the cobblestone with its singular joy
and shreds the map I'm holding in my hands.

ANDERSON

Fucks my throat

Adjusts his hips and tries to stick

His unwrapped cock inside me

Naw, man

He tells me he will shower and that he'll be right back

We both know he is lying

My reflection passes his reflection

In the bathhouse's mirrored hallways

As if both of us were walking

The passageway from this world

Into the next together

I leave the building

My boyfriend half a world away

Ignoring texts because he doesn't like what's in them

I'm thinking of Anderson's cock

On the cobbled slope of the Travessa dos Fiéis de Deus

His cock that is small

Yet thick and powerful

Something I could slide in and out of my body

Like I could the barrel of a gun

Roses for fuckboys

Bairro Alto sweats

Cut-out men approach me, offer ersatz cocaine

A mix of powdered glue and baking soda

July moon shivering with fever

The men exploding into pigeons

Wearing little backpacks

Full of ecstasy

THE HEART OF THE TOURIST IS EMPTY

I

To travel the world inside your own dumbass skull
And not disturb a single neuron in it
As last looks go you could do worse
Than a tower of flame

II

The sky is mouldy peach
I am drawn to this evil pier
Its lignified steps
Wet with stinking dulse
You have your self-destructing instructions
Meet me at the gate where air meets water
Break only hearts, take only photographs

III

Men are beasts! always
Piss on the seat always
Shouting slack-jawed always
Stuffing their cocks
In your mouth

IV

I see the girls walk by dressed in their summer colds

V

Lightning strikes the top of the greenhouse
Again and again I experience
Sensation x
And x engenders pain in the world
Therefore I engender pain
        A bolt from the blues

VI

I follow him up to the man-made waterfall
Ass testing the seams of his twill pants
I want so badly for our bodies to communicate
A spirit tricks me into the eastern grotto
Magic is happening here
My good bitch

VII

In the kitchen hot milk
Hits boiled ginger juice
Curdles into skin
A barrier that air cannot traverse

VIII

One perfect white specimen left on a rotting rosebush
Two beetles hidden, fucking inside it
The heart of the tourist is empty

IX

Crackle of fish skin
Time to throw another thing on the fire
A man vomits into a dumpster
Wipes his mouth
Cheers
The dumpster cheers too!

X

THE ROSE GARDEN IS A MISNOMER

XI

Still pool
Surrounding a rose garden of your own
Carefully manicured
Hybridized
Reflection
Repose
Branding
Solitude
Delusion
Ad nauseam

XII

Hot ginger milk
Curdling on my face

HAVING EXACTLY ALL OF IT

Airports give me the jinkies, I'll admit
helped none by my chauffeur's palaver
about baseball on the hour-long drive
from Wilmington to Philly
so I was not exactly shocked the fervent
TSA agent asked me to spread 'em,

remove my emerald cufflinks. What did surprise:
my cock, hot, animate, as he frisked
the inseam of my Junya Watanabe

slacks. Humiliating crescendo to
the mirthless bleep-boops of the body scanners.
So intimate. No man had touched me there since you

nine weeks ago. I had not, prior to
my unscheduled tumescence, thought about

your hand inside my body for a firm twenty-seven hours.
No one comes to Delaware for pleasure.
At liftoff, despite tonic of Xanax, cold-pressed

prune juice with Himalayan pink
salt rim, I feel hollow as the corporations
Mother's fortune was subdivided into

with names like Solvetica LLC. Cruising: a hard choice
between Strega-poached chicken ballotine
or manicotti with escargot demi-glace,

but I can't stomach absence. I'd scramble
a Fabergé egg if you'd
pour candle wax on my nipples again
remain the canker to my apple, lancet
to my throbbing boil. The stewardess
offers a moist towelette to wipe away what remains unsaid.

I accept, knowing when I pull into the Bridle Path
the only thing I own is
the shell game of an empty master bedroom
cold marble countertops, a bowl of peaches bearded with mould.

STEAMWORKS

After Marcus McCann

Limbs sweated alembic, salt lick–wet
skewing gravity centres, slick torsos
akimbo. Adonic triad keys voltaic gates.
Mouthmulching, hirsute individual flips
mirrored ceiling into sauna panelling.
Lazily equate a fluid sacrament,
spit the margarine to grease the crack
that's in the world. Spacious voids
expand gestures. Sit pretty, servile
in fraggled syntax: I walk to the edge.
But every single time I let myself walk back.

ADVENTURE TIME I

The Craigslist post requested two
boys: bushy-tailed, chipmunk-cheeked

pure hearts, yadda yadda. We struck
camp at daybreak in a hamlet

where Churchill's voice is still
tonic as brandy. I love you but

we need to find clean water
and a flower that blooms

with the fragrance of mischief. I don't or can't
tell you about the men I think I'm kissing

before I've fully woken up. I'm not asking
for a love spell, just its shadow word: *commitment.*

When we speak of things worth doing
we're not talking about risk, I've tried

Advil and the almanac,
stuck my dad's gemsteel machete

in the mouth of your tributary
but the beach was needled with Irukandji stingers.

And if I fall victim to enchantment? Visions
of other lives spent with other bodies,

the subtle glamers of crème de violette.
Consulted a friendly teenaged haruspex

and she ripped a wet fistful
of entrails, orange with Easy Mac.

This is, at best, a neutral omen.
But we can make this work. I do it

for you: be a conduit. Interpret
the letter of the lightning:

that everything that enters exits
into this undiscovered country.

AFTER EIGHT

After you fisted me
without written consent I thought to ask
you to go the distance, yank out the steel wool ball

scouring my thorax. *Wow, your hands,*
scalding water, *what an inappropriate thing*
to ask of a total stranger, scrubbing away all traces

of irony. And tonight we eat fish
'cuz it's Friday, Filet-O if you're nasty.
In all seriousness I brought you a little skate

wing crusted with scorched salt and a little mint.
Look at it: gelatinous, white. It's trying
to fly away from you, I said, but it can't

because it's dead and the burnt salt is not
a ruined cloud. *Cut it out,* you said.
So I took the knife to my Gordian knot instead.

After dinner I wiped olive oil from your eyes.
The heart when drained of blood is the colour of salt.
You held the sun in your hands; it shivered

like a little mammal. It's fine, darling,
everything's fine. Put the kettle on.
Let's watch a little TV. It's a documentary

about a drunk man kicking an otter to death
in the middle of the street you grew up on.
I laughed and a little jet of blood

shot from my mouth
into your eye. How embarrassing.
Please, let's not do this here, you said.

What an inappropriate thing to say
to a stranger. Either your dad's dead
or you'd like him to be. That summer you

got conjunctivitis. I grew mint in a little pot,
but it was the hottest summer on record –
every summer was the hottest summer on record –
so the mint dried into rust.

KELETI STATION

> I'm practically in a state of shock because of what I did
> and what has been done to me … I panic, now as I'm
> watching the footage it's like it wasn't even me.
> *— Petra László (translated by Mariann Óry)*

> There is no fundamental right to a better life.
> *— Viktor Orbán, prime minister of Hungary*

First you came for the far-right camerawomen,
and I did not speak out, for I was not a fuckwit.
Now, watching the footage, it's like a foreign film
I watched as a child in a dream, a soundtrack
of moonlight with occasional cicada.
You washed the streets clean, swept Romani
into dusty little corners of former industrial cities,
sold fresh cabbage and carrots on Kazinczy Street.
A culture is absolutely worth defending:
I, for instance, just tossed my ex's
sourdough starter fermenting on the fridge
six weeks after he left. The radical choice is
a population as pasty and refined as lángos.
It's like it wasn't even me, turista in jackboots
on the dance floor, sucking back fény and complicity.
There is no fundamental right to a better life, of course
but you reserve the right to scrape the grout off Oktogon.
Is that the Halászbástya you'd like to die on?
Well, perhaps not, but the better to
enjoy your meal at the Andrássy Burger King that way,
under a sky expressionless and cold as a denied visa.
Silent, now. I hear the coming of a train.

KREUZBERG

The blond Australian's jaw is clenched in ecstasy. His jaw
is clenched as though to say I'm having so much fun
you can see it in my face. With a *kshink!* I pass
my retractable claws right through his thorax.
He hugs me. His sweat is stale battery acid.

In the capital, cultural capital is the only capital.
That's why the bank has repossessed my studio
in the eternal mortgage crisis of the present.
In the world to come, manufacturers come and go
talking about debt-to-earnings ratio.

Wherever the jobs aren't
that's where I fly to.
That's how I produce my art.
Dessert in economy class is a Lampedusan blood gelée.
Dessert in this fourth-wave café
is a neighbourhood gnashing its teeth
for yarn shops and strollers and whiteness to swoop in.
I work on commission for Lockheed Martin.
The name of this neighbourhood means Christberg,
which is an absolute dud in need of a rebrand.
History slithers in mysterious bands.
Red touches yellow touches black.
Every man in Xberg (née Kreuzberg) has identical tattoos.
It's 2022 and they are rounding up the homeless,
soon the trans girls, then the faggots too.

Raytheon market cap soaring.
All my wars are foreign.
Condos all new flooring.
Bombs arc over Golan.

EQUINOX

Last night
In a Berlin McDonald's I watched
A woman nod out standing up
Her scrunchy filthy pink
Her large boyfriend snapping at her
And thought, Will I be good? Would I
Save this stranger's life? Tonight?
      Instead my phone looked into me
Until the paramedics came. I composed myself
And ate a hamburger the size of my face
Will I remember that hamburger forever?

      It is the transience of pleasure
      That makes pleasure dangerous

You cannot have the life you want.
You will create pain
In yourself and others.
The expressed joy
Of purple loosestrife
We call invasive.
This is a problem of poetry

My bourgeois grandma
Told me a story
About a girl who loved music
But wished that time
Would stop forever
So she wouldn't have to do her homework
The thesis of the story being
Without time passing
There can be no motion

Motion being a series
Of records against and within time
And without motion no music
Music being the physic of
A ratio of time divided by motion
A world without music
Would be a tragedy
Who am I to disagree

But even as a child I knew this was wrong:
A universe without time is
Just light
The white of the light of every star in the universe
And cold because
Without time passing
There can be no motion
And therefore no heat
The music the frozen
Chord of every
Note played everywhere
At once and without decay
I'm sorry but
I don't make the rules
This is what the dreamers call heaven
It has practical and material consequences
For life on earth
I'm sorry but
Utopia isn't a place
It's a feeling

The sound of two mirrors reflecting
Plays an awful tune

[ASSETS NOW IN PLAY]

In cotton white briefs   Bodies flagrant discomposing

Dishonourable discharges   From the ER

Hospital fluorine   Took too much hash, ended up there

Again   And the album playing on the hospital speakers

Is a little cheesy   Sounds like it's

"Going to Ibiza"   And we say

We say Never Again   And God suggests

Nobody gets to say that   Without a test of their resolve

And so we say

Ibiza is not the Carthage we did not want to burn

Ibiza is not the Rome you sought for

Ibiza and Berlin too are assets now in play

So decode secret instructions in the Morse code of a catheter

Look out the window. The dead hang there

Tearless on black oaks lacquered now in rain

Dripping as my hands do   Now of opaque rain …

I could speak of it only

Via negation

A story the mind tells the body

In the body's secretions, written in

A script the mind cannot read

Does not register

In the part of the mind corresponding to language

And in this hospital there is no picture we could take

Of the space around a molecule

Vibrating in a magnetic field

To produce for us the comfort of a diagnosis

In this hospital, we discern grand and terrible truths.

It's not all that we discern from each other

It's not all that I want to describe

I wanted to describe the feeling of electric

Current that I regarded as the root of the word *venir*

To come – a hairy fleshy sort of romance

Unmediated by a screen

Was still, as of today's writing, still possible

If only at an instant of connection

Even at this blue-black hour I find myself in

Historical materialism feels insufficient

When between the crackle of energy expressed by two bodies

Displayed on the sanitized iPad stations with which

We see off our dead

                              In the most noble fashion our culture affords us

HALL OF A HUNDRED REFLECTIVE SURFACES

A boy home
Undressed.
Ribs of beaten greyhound,
Breath of beaten greyhound.
Not dead.
As cold.

Cold as Lapland!!! Cold
Pills in a marble pestle.
Pill frost in ice water.
Wind's razor pressures a single vein.
A hundred mirrors in the house
Not one returns the gauntness in his grin

The hands go slack in opiate flow
Hail has smacked the hands a hundred times.
A hundred times he fumbles chunks of ice
But cannot spell out *anodyne*

Give us, O Lord, our daily pardons.
He guides my fingers underneath his ribs
He lets me put my fingers in his wound
He shows me how his liver hardens

WASTED

I got into in-patient
She smiles bone-dry
Caliper the fat on my hard palate
Her skeleton grimaces
I scrape a little mould off some cheddar with a butter knife
I am so happy in uncomplicated ways these days
A sun salutation expels exactly sixteen calories
The goose's neck bruised from the cascade of apples down its feeding tube
So happy for her in uncomplicated ways
It is often the ambitious ones
But I recovered years ago
Scraping whipped topping off my non-fat dairy dessert
I hope this isn't triggering for you, she says
I'm at my highest weight ever but I'm fine, who's counting anyway
It's all I think about, she says
No, no, smiling
Your fridge is beautiful
I drizzle ganache out my mouth into the waste bin
Smile the colour of orange pekoe sweetened with saccharin
I scrape the back of my throat with a buttered knife
The vomit is decadent   It circles the drain

SILVER NEEDLE TEA

In a city cold as a syringe
He serves me silver needle tea.
Prefers I not stare at his track marks
When he's in shirtsleeves.
I let the powder wash down my tongue
So I never have to feel this way again.
The world ended a decade ago;
We're just waiting for the confirmation email.
Here every home's a million-dollar teardown
With a basement full of dime bags.
Here the traffic lights wink green, whispering to you
That with enough money, you could be anybody.
You could drive straight through
All night if you like.
You're in the driver's seat.
Nobody can force you to stop
Or slow down.
Go far
And as fast
As you like

KISS FROM A ROSE

I saw my own face in the topology of the rose's corolla.
The stem drew blood, and in the drop
the universe passed out through me and into itself.
True: we can say a rose is not a zero-sum game.

Under the material conditions of living
its roseness abandons it.
Yet its rosedom remains.

The soil grows hurt in the guise of a thorn.
Someone once nursed this blue
bouquet of bruises, freshly cut.
My mother gathered roses with her hair all shorn.

I wanted a sign. Nothing too obvious
or heavy-handed, because those kinds
of messages from God
really tend to freak me out.
But still I needed something
which said, authoritatively
that something does remain of the rose
after every petal is burned ...

PROTECTIVE WEIRDING

The night purrs. I'm liquored
slick with gin and camphor.
Your arm with the left-handed
swastika tattoo, scruff of my neck,
I'm groomed. Dogteeth smile.
Now who's a good boy.
A very good boy. You say

I had no idea you were so young;
I interpret this as a compliment.
My eighteenth birthday. Your gift –

draped crystal and chain over my nape.
To protect me from all harm
done by others. I did not scan

the emphasis. I dropped my
twenty-sided die; failed fortitude
save against charisma.

In a pawnshop, eight years later,
I get the gift appraised: not crystal
at all. Set in lead and storm glass:

little ampoule of fox urine. A mark:
scentless in the cold of a crowd
unbearable musk
when an older man got me
alone in a warm room.

BOTTLED

The air dry as gin.
Peggy Lee plays in this dive bar we sleep in:
"Is that all there is?"

I know you hear it, Calvin:
I hear it in the kick of gravel in your throat
when you tell me you've been boiled
every evening since last March.

It slipped in –
something that doesn't love at all
through blistered palms
spading ash saplings for four cents a unit –
something old and hungry in the yew.

Something old and hungry wearing your skin in the morning.
Your cheeks that owned a rosedom
now as red as the bloat of hibiscus stewed in gin.
Hair as flax as a minor Polish saint;
a back that ripples in the shine of the moon.
I always hoped if I were beautiful
I wouldn't need these altered states.
But things that are are not the things we think.
Hi, I'm Jake. It's been two hundred days since my last drink.

Calvin, life's so much worse than I suspected.
Here's some benzos for the shakes.
Please take only as directed.

HEIR CONSUMPTIVE

It was the year of the asp
fellating its own tail, year of
opioid-induced constipation

I slept with fangs on the wink
of your scrotum. I shat out your bones
and whittled 'em into fountain pens.

Give me Librium, or give me meth. I knew
you play-acted the way your cousin puppeted you
when he was twenty and you were ten

They found him in a white van on Stanley and Jane,
a bullet snaked in his sphincter
out his brain. How, even then,

steel wool couldn't scour the stench
from my hands. How, even then,
the semaphore of my cigarette

relayed your halfway house's
hidden location. How, even then,
if snitches get stitches, that a pound

of your flesh binds my debut collection.
How apology's sweet, but never so sugared
as the liquid the clinic dispenses at ten.
How daily I swallow my medicine.

HOW SHOULD A PERSON BE?

Some things magic cannot fix.
The magician drops the hazel switch,
the dazzling sapphire cape, cuts the shit,
reveals himself to be the speaker of this poem.

The speaker of this poem apologizes
because some people have real problems
and he merely had needs that were not validated.

The speaker of this poem displays
the door to nothingness under his rib cage.
The speaker of the poem admits
that nothing he had tried could ever bar it,
the door – not water-cooler chats; nor mascfag body;

nor substituted amphetamines; nor epinephrine; nor art;
nor DBT; nor Westvleteren 12, nor "purpose";
nor strawberry-flavoured dick; nor raw candy. The speaker

of this poem is hollow, so picture the speaker
the first six weeks of his life, as a two-pound infant
moulting in an incubator, caressed by needlepoint
his mother's hands against a pane of jaundiced glass.

There, now. The show is over.
Please hold your applause if you can.
I'm the speaker. Probably why

I cannot feel you when you hold me

A KINDNESS

This bathhouse had red walls and the smell of fungal death
And these like … train compartment
"Fucking booths" with upholstery stuffing
And horizontal sliding doors
> Like a train compartment
> The Bobbsey Twins slept inside
> On some old-timey book jacket illustration in my mind …

Where Ben laid one hand flat on top of my chest
Then punched it hard with his other one
So that I felt the punch's impact
But not the sting
Thank you, Ben
That's kind of you
That is a kindness
> That you gave to me
> When you didn't need to
May I call you Benjamin?
I have already called you Daddy
I have already called you Sir
I'm interested in domination
But not pain, said Ben.
I have no use for pain,
Said Ben

Thank you, Ben. That's kind of you.
But I do have a use for pain.
I suck it up like milkshake
I vomit it onto
Your kitchen floor
It dries   The residue
Forms the shape of pretty words

CHICKEN HYPNOTISM

Kelvin walked down the stairs
To take what was his
And what was his was my body

When he came down my throat
His thighs and torso seized
Like the painting of a man I've seen
In the grips of tetanus
I did not care if we were caught
I did not care about anything
But my duty
Because I know my worth now
I can feel it in my heart
And I can suspend it
Temporarily   Voluntarily
There was only one time
I didn't suspend it willingly
And every time I do now, I take revenge against you, Elliott
Every bottom in my hometown city shudders
When your name is spoken
But now I have my revenge, Elliott
Now I say your name to my book
I write it down
I curse your offspring, Elliott
Your parents wither in front of you, Elliott
You live in their basement
Your every joy turns to nothingness, Elliott
Your joy is the pale moon to my sun
Because you had to steal your every joy
And I gave every joy
To anyone that asked
And to each of them I gave my joy willingly

Even this is to overstate
Your gravity
Aside from today
In my notebook
And in all the other poems I've written about it
I think of you hardly ever at all
Instead, I think of chicken hypnotism
And how you can stun any chicken
Into a calm, compliant state
By suddenly clapping your hands in its face

CLOUD OF UNKNOWING

Things change.
Sugar is now a listed toxin.
I stick a cube of it under my tongue.
You can make jam if you leave blood in the sun.
The mirrors of empty million-dollar flats arranged in a ring
Focus the rays of the sun on the flammable cladding
That cocoons the subsidized housing tower.
Archimedes sets the Roman ships ablaze.
This brings new clarity to the phrase *the war on poverty*.
The mirror of time spins into fifty million rolling heads
My eyes the rounded rims of gold cups.
It's hard to concentrate because this world is a shifting, buzzing thing. But we must.
Even as we stare into a sky of smoke congealed into the violet of a day-old bruise.
My mother told me my mind was a dirty mirror
But I know no surface reflects like fire.
So hold my hand. We must move fast. Grab only what you need.
The tower between this world and the next is being built
That's why it hurts this much to live here, and to bleed.

I SAW A MAN I VAGUELY WANTED

I saw a man I vaguely wanted
Smoking on a concrete planter
An open sore like a USB port
Amid his monochrome tattoos

If you are not wearing
The proscribed colours here
You must be questioned by the authorities
They will pry you open with their
Long batons

A white woman dressed in shades of taupe and cream
Was wearing a Christian Dior sun hat
Retail price ten thousand dollars
She was swaying   Hands clasped
In time to the music
The young Black singer sang to
The singer's voice was beautiful
I saw the way the woman in the sun hat looked at him
I saw love in her eyes. I saw hope
Glisten like gold on Oxford Street
I wanted to believe in her
I swear I wanted to believe

YOU COULD BE FORGIVEN

Wearing the signature scent for
"Could you please bring the cheque"
Gulls at twilight overhead

"Exciting New Brand Opening Soon"
And no consideration for those of us
Left behind here

You could be forgiven
For thinking all this
Looked like fun

THE SUN HAS NEVER LOOKED SO LARGE

I just did monogamy
At the sex party
I only had sex with two people in four hours
The sun on the train blinded me
I looked right at it
There was a crescent within its light
Now I see nothing

Richard's dick
His beautiful, beautiful dick
He was very concerned with, apologetic about not cumming
But I too take SSRIs

He was so worried
That I could have had anyone at the sex party that I wanted
He did not notice I had not chosen
Anyone else I could have had

And what was most significant in all of it
The high horse chestnut spangling anons
I mean spanning aeons
I mean spinning irons I mean
The most significant thing was
The spilled Maltesers in the vending machine
On the train platform on my way home
An explosion of brown globules or spheres
An explosion that didn't move
Suspended or preserved in air
My mind returns often to the Maltesers …
My mind orbits the Maltesers suspended in air …

Like so many moons orbiting a large, large ball
Of swirling gas
That is not on fire

I swear the sun has never looked so large
The sun now setting
Over Empire

HUGE PAYLOAD

At six on the shitter:
Anal-retentive, I promised to God
I would be Good
So long as nobody that I loved ever had to die
Well, I mostly kept my end of the bargain …

I trusted love and love
Sodomized me
Empathy wore me
Bedraggled

And my heart is so wide open, baby
Open and poisonous as poetry
Stop to sniff the foxglove too long
And your heart stops there with you

God doesn't exist
The way we'd like God to
Or can understand and that
That is enough

About that particular subject
I am rich with feelings. Waking already
On the other side of the veil of ignorance
Clothed in the thin gauze of genocide
Counterpoint of birdsong against cold sunrise
Hungover from the party of a lifetime

You asked me to bring you
Something you could relate to

It isn't hard to bring yourself to another world
To live somewhere you've never lived

Wake up in a war you've never seen
On television. I wanted them to die –

The singing birds
Their music keeps me from my sleep

MASSIVE ORDNANCE AIR BLAST I

Ignorance is how I keep living.
No human language can withstand the speed of light.

My complicity in this consumes
air dancing in my lungs. An impulse is a power in itself.

Maybe you saw the finger of God
or Empire jab a tongue depressor hard

the firmament sneezed, the dust kicked up
and lit on fire. A tally is kept and erased daily.

Zero days since mass murder last
paid for my ostensible freedoms. A shirtless man

jogs his body by me on the street, a testament
to the transformational powers of suffering.

Each receive our countless blessings.
These are boons that beg

for a balm. May the war bring you peace.
Please refrain from refraining.

We do not deserve it,
this high cost of living.

HOW PERILOUS IS PURITY OF HEART

To celebrate surviving the Beer Hall Putsch,
I bought America a bouquet of blue roses.
One whole dozen, at full expense. Hooray!

Jimmy Breslin called Rudy Giuliani a small man in search of a balcony.
Some small men live in search of a bunker.
Some men fuck you by writing an email containing an hourly rate and suite number.
Some men fuck you while wearing lace hosiery. Who cares!

Some small men fuck you and put a condom on after.
Some men became ash.
Some men had toxic scrunge fall on them after.
All men are in search of a rope and a rafter.

Rudy Giuliani, America's mayor, reduced to riding in coach!
I bet Rudy Giuliani has an asshole that looks
like a gassed cockroach.

My hairdresser said all men search for absolution,
but small men search for a world free and clear.
I am told Mouton Rothschild '46 is an exceptional year.
If you squint, you can see the smoke from here.

FOUR-MINUTE WARNING

My body has been compromised by a foreign power
Unsuspecting actor for the deep state

Explosion bubbles onto pink Formica counter
Extremities curl up involuntarily

To shield my torso from
Frisson of matter meeting uncontainable force

I am no atomic playboy accomplishing strategic invectives
Pinned by amyl nitrite under the collapsible boardroom table

He rams into me like I am subcritical uranium
In a gun-type fission weapon ashen in colour

I drool into his snapped limb on the seafoam shag carpet
So many bodies atomized for my ability to do this

Pinkwash wherever the war is
Wherever the bomb goes: pink mist

The virus enters the cell with a lubed flagellum
With a gentle bloom on the grey screen Hellfire enters the hospital

Legs tremble from the distant blast I fall
To my knees to slurp Capitalism's sloppy seconds

Full payload tears open my jaw
I say, "Thank you, Daddy," to Daddy Warbucks

Dropping you, my love, from the cockpit
Your body moves away from me so quickly
Another thousand feet per second

THE BOMB IS THE BUDDHA OF THE WEST

On waking I resolve to meet the world with perfect information.
The sun this morning was the Castle Bravo test explosion.

Ko Un poured acid in his ear
so he wouldn't hear his cellmates tortured.
As I contemplate the rising figure on my digital bathroom scale,
forty-two children are murdered by Hellfire missiles.
What is Heaven in virtue of the bomb?

The perfect information of a mountain is corrupted
by the drift of a passing cirrostratus.

At the base of the missile silo, my asshole and mouth
form a sixty-eight-member strategic alliance.
You could call it the mother of all coalitions.
The rate of capital expansion lulls.
Little Boy's blast echoes in my skull.

I greet the light directly and it craves my imperfection.
Compassion is the means the light employs.

'Cuz *bomb*'s such an old-fashioned word.
Listen – someone now is passing through
from the other side.

ON THE THIRTY-NINTH DAY OF RAIN

I've lived thirty years in this wasting stalk
and nobody bothered to give a tour. On Wednesdays

we wear thin. God unzips me and slides in.
It rains milk of mag inside

the Stamford offices of Purdue Pharma. It rains
tamper-proof capsules over Ohio. It rains

without a smile in Niamey, Houston, Mumbai, Tallahassee,
San Juan. Ceilings rush to meet rising water, kiss bloodied mouths.

My mother's evening lullaby takes the shape
of a hollowed-out Javex bottle.

I scoop storms out the silty bottom of our lifeboats.
Find my body slumped over holding a still-unlit blueberry scone.

They thought us downwinders. They thought they could
leave us behind. That high tides only sink ships lacking

virtue or assets, but water's or greed's only limit is
the size of their containers. I have a million bodies

screaming inside my body. A year is also a vase
and can contain any amount of suffering

glazed with roses. God took me
so many places already, with sand sublimated into glass,

with shadows vaporized into the walls. I just want to stay
where I am. Batten down the hatches.

I thirst for water that streams out your body.
My tears pooling into the dirt floor of this abandoned research facility –

Weepy me   my gloomy dooms
my hot pocket   my hard mantle of stars
my deep dark dreams   my matte bronze powders

WINDOWS XP FOR OHIO-CLASS SUBMARINES

On shore leave in Rio
dreaming of OxyContin,
dental floss a rose's stem between my teeth.
Contempt is the first step to acceptance.
As far as the eye can see, it sees nothing.
A time is coming when nothing is easy, but everything's free.
Sleep requires I show my papers nightly.

We called this place a country
but it was only the moon
searing the cold fjord,
a flock of brant geese in flux.
An opening salvo.
A brief convalescence.
The terminal secretions of capital.
Where could we go? The leaves were red with fire.
Finding love the higher law
we transfigured our love into weapons
and we learned to love the payload.

I could never throw roses to Hitler.
We called this place a city but a city was something more
than polyps of shattered courtyards
the grave markers of phone booths,
postcards crying for the incinerator,
more than the fattening silence of bombs.

My dad, green from mowing the lawn, didn't remember the Cold War.
I asked him to shut up and hold me,
and tell me everything would be fine in a dad way
and to tell me a story. And he told me

that in the dark heart of the ash forest
was a still lake where the moon's reflection
was cold and large as the moon itself,
and in the lake an islet
with a lichen-covered grotto
that flooded in the night,

and if you took a little wooden boat to sail
you could pull up a bucket from the well
you could draw up the pure clay of your heart
and watch the clay pour through your hands.

PACIFIC THEATRE

TRANS-PACIFIC

With a sourness growing in my mouth
Silently like a canker or
Death cap mushroom but really
I need to brush my teeth
An interminable five hours remain suspended
Above the earth in a shellacked metal tube
A sight to stopper ancient women's hearts
But there is nothing that a human being cannot
Grow to take for granted. Younger I pondered
How the films, fashions, forms and funs
Of my contemporary moment would ever feel
As old as "olden days" but time
Insidiously paints a patina of disgust on even
The most beloved of film franchises.
Soon even my treasured and esteemed
"DADDYs abuse cumdump in hotel"
Pornhub HD recording would
Be as mottled, aged and worn with sunspots
As the face and cock that gazed lovingly upon it.
Strange painful fluid pooling in the bending of my knee
Where I reclined over the Arctic Ocean ice
And Anchorage, Alaska, where our plane would cast
A looming shadow over Sarah Palin's house
Made famous by Tina Fey on *SNL*.
                    How's that for a dated reference.
I had time to kill.
Time was killing me, but deadly slowly.
It was something about the light that betrayed the age of the films.
I suppose the light betrayed my age as well.
The age betrayed its paeans and pablums to

Common decency and trust in institutions.
Moneyed elderly people waggled their tongues at me.
Had I become a demagogue? Maybe so.
But these truths appeared to me self-evident.
And with age becomes harder to ignore
Like the funk in Rocquefort
And this painful fluid pooling in my knee.
Knocking past Petropavlovsk-Kamchatsky.
Where was Timbuktu anyway, and why
Had so many fiends and villains gotten themselves shipped
There in inescapable wooden crates?
Time had brought me here
To resent the things I once professed to love
And to have become the things I once professed
To have resented. These vapid excursions
Gay Lycra wear   Would I ever shut up
About fucking. Probably not. "Getting more
Of our valuable natural resources to global markets."
The only currency the market traded in was death
And I said that as a beneficiary to these

            Just deserts   Earthly delights
Turkish or otherwise   Bye for now

[THE GLOAMING CUT LIKE A WARM KNIFE INTO A SACHERTORTE OVER THE PACIFIC]

The gloaming cut like a warm knife into a Sachertorte over the Pacific
A woman livestreaming her manic episode
Gloating about her lack of need for sleep
Her "superwpoers" [*sic*]
Perhaps the finished album was to be that good
It was difficult to discern this over Facebook Stories
My second boyfriend furious
Would not admit it
His anger was justified
But so was mine
Some tournaments have no clear victor
In the contest of love I took pleasure
In acquisition and becoming then
Aloof   Cold   Unattached
In variegated shades
In degrees of weight and form
Over the Pacific
The RCMP "E" Division stormed
Into Unist'ot'en camp
While I unwrapped onigiri with umeboshi
Purchased at the 7-Eleven with money partially financed by
The Canadian tar sands   The banks that
Financed them
Drinking tap water stolen
By the food + bevg
Industry   Encased in plastic
Produced by the petroleum by-products industry
In a country that also had   Raped, massacred, enslaved
That I had been transported to   In an aircraft
Constructed and designed   By the weapons manufacturing industry

It was difficult to
Extract oneself   As minerals were
From what surrounded one   One could run away
If one tried   And if one could afford it
    But never too long   Never long enough
No matter where   You remained on planet Earth
The only true company   One's inadequate self
Travel promises   Freedom but
It too is illusion.
        Only death awaits

TO THE GENERATIVE POWER OF THE

Prancing through the megalopolis viewing
Clothing that costs more than my rent
If one isn't careful the world sucks one
Back in   with a shudder
    As a sphincter does
When a cock does move beyond it
Back into a savoury experience of alienation
Compensative xenophobia acid reflux rising
Past the ring of flesh that seals the esophagus shut
And I know all too well   Being Canadian
How fatal it can be   To ever mistake politeness for decency
Acidulated roses in the air   Plum blossom debris
Some pear flowers   I swear to you
On the lives of my three grandmothers
Smell exactly like just-shot cum
Hot, mineral, saline
A metallic salt   "At this late stage" I was
An atom of potassium   Ready to give it up
To just about anyone who came along
I was thinking these very pure and pristine thoughts
At the war atrocities museum
Photos of things I ought not describe here
Stolen wounds and septic futures
But if I spare a tear for these innocents
Do the tears redeem the nation that produced them
Do the tears redeem mine?
There are innocent people   I want to believe
But perhaps no innocent peoples
All lays flat across time's big butcher's block
Bludgeoning board   His abacus of bones

His zither strung with viscera

The average fool thought of death just once a week

I guess I was more foolish than average

I saw misfortune in every suit of the deck

But I was happier now to accept my inexorable fate

Could be a happy fool   Cartwheeling through the doorway to oblivion

Drinking an organic lemon soda in the forest

In the eastern centre of the megalopolis

Coins falling from my person

Hairs falling from my scalp

What I take with me into the steam room

Rising to meet the power in my little body

Heart a-burstin' with life   I can't affirm

I have no fear of death   But now my fear is not the same

Women in smart woollen sweaters

Charming, demure women with beautiful hair

Genki drinks   A nation of men with

Gorgeous asses and spindly legs   A racist generalization overtakes me

Like a horny mood   Like I count evil cows

In my grubby hands   Elsewhere a family was massacred today

You could set your watch by it   An atomic clock

Dung beetle of the sun   Rising up on its hindquarters

About to burrow into the earth

POEM FOR KEN

Is this a love poem? I do not write love poetry
Do not know how
Am motivated to the page
Primarily by anxiety, despair
Occasionally a vicarious mood of luxury. But never love
Which is too intense, too fleeting.
I get swept up in its refrains.
Besides, I did not love you. We did not have time.
It would not have worked if we did.
I already have two boyfriends and live a world away.
I prefer triangulation. Cannot take satisfaction in one body.
Not even my own. You long for a stable dyad
And will chase it in the unlikeliest of figures.
Such as the travelling polyamorous Canadian.
Whereas I believe that hunger is the choicest seasoning
Followed only by novelty.
Then this obsequious service.
This strangely flavoured chiffon cake.
A more palatable form of luxury.
I feel like an open sore.
But I will not feel that way forever.
Acid rises in my throat at the thought of one more day
To communicate my being to others only with
A single phrase: *Thank you so much,*
Arigato gozaimas.
But, Ken, thank you so much.
You should really go to therapy.
The upbringing in a notorious cult – saved that one for the third date
Slipped it in nonchalantly. Would I try
Monogamy for you? No. This is the way I am.

Ask anybody. Ask Graeme, David, David, Daniel, Luis,
Luis, Jeremy, Tyler, Paul, Paul, Jason, Kenny, Jake,
Ed, Chon, Moon Jung, Mathieu, Marco, Luke
And Jon. And *those* are just the last six months
And those I got the names of.
Time and space. Relativity and distance.
Biochemicals and circumstances.
But I can say I loved you all the same
And that there is nothing as nice
As having loved someone I never could claim

NOTHING EVER DOES

Scenes of court dancers and jesters
Gilded oak leaves
Halberds

Ritual bells
Thousand-year-old swords lost to time's edge
Verdigris

One truth remains across centuries:
The collection of beautiful objects
Is incompatible with virtue

Maybe that truth could bring a happiness
A warmth.
It doesn't last
For nothing ever does

EN ROUTE TO ZOSHIGAYA STATION

Cosmetics for foreigners
Evil burnt-sugar aroma
Schoolgirls chowing down on cheese corn dogs

Now they're gone
What a thrill

To be hungry and alive in February
Wash yourself here and be purified

A powerful mallard
Glides into a fountain

I was ready to commit to revolutionary action
After this brief shopping interlude

Your indigent reporter
Diligently sending viewers back home

A floral cherry cola
Visions of a spring to come

KEN

The veins in his hand as he writes the sushi order

All we have in this life are our
Little loves devoured by time's
Gaping mouth

How arrogant was I to
Want to write my name down in its stomach

Bronze swords no edge could maintain

A molecule of oxytocin
Moving from my gut to cock to brain

Plum blossoms falling in rain

A subway tunnel crumbling on a train

The fire we stoke between our hands

Once handsome and tall as you

INFINITE CRYSTAL UNIVERSE

Transfixed by the
Beauty of my image
With scintillating lights
How could I resist
A hall of gilded mirrors
All of us staring upwards
At the simulation of a universe of light

With this in mind I turned toward a screen

Captive Apple
Glinting in the winter sun

Kawaii image of a miniature dachshund dog
Choked by its leash in an elevator door

Finding parallels between the life
I believed myself to live
And the ones I imagined the people here did
Us   and   Them
But there was nothing but the pleasure
Of alienation I'd willingly subjected myself to

At great expense
To myself
The planet
And the ecosystem

KYOTO

Cormorant gulp silver koi whole
Narcissi with heads bowed under the weight of their own thoughts
An embarrassment of riches

Crowned night heron
Silver rain tearing the prayer paper
I could not tell if it were a darkened tree-covered mountain before me
Or a monstrous cloud that would unload on me
Or end me

I craved. I sought pleasure
No sooner had I beheld it
In my grubby little hands
I despised and castigated myself for it
My "forbidden night coffee"

Sacrum spasms   In my back muscles
The colour of spoiled milk   Clotting
Because my back was unaccustomed to bowing
Unaccustomed to showing deference   In comparison to
My apparent idea of "the Japanese"
Racist fantasia   Fantasy of a unified culture
Or vision   How many times have I told you
The heart of the tourist is empty

Caterwauling away   Shopping and dining
During an important moment
In my nation's genocidal history
The RCMP points guns at Indigenous people
To enable the sale of natural resources

Which I could only witness from afar   And on my telephone
Buying souvenirs   "Below memory"
As the pigs marched into the camps
And got happy, flopping in the muck and oil
Pools of melted slag, bright hot on a dark grey hill

I watch the contents of a McDonald's bag explode
Into the air as it is struck by a passing bus
Fries fly onto the sidewalk in slow motion

A TASTE FOR PUFFERFISH

In a city of manners I can't understand

My friend and I splurged on a nice ryokan, the price of which

For a single night was twice my monthly share of rent

And my friend, not wanting to seem rude or impolite

In such an upscale establishment, burned herself

In the bath they drew for her when we checked in

Made herself ill from the heat of the steam

Could not enjoy the luxurious, ten-course kaiseki meal she'd paid for

And accompanying lesson on what kaiseki is

Designed for tourists like the two of us

Who have no appreciation for

The art form or its long imperial history.

And since my friend was socialized as female, and I as male

I just ran the cold water and opened the window

There are a few things I permit myself to do without asking.

The meal was fantastic

The service impeccable, old-fashioned

I did not think about the labour costs

Or the political economy behind it for

A single instant, although it was late February 2020

What was notable about the dinner

Was the fact I was served a dish of fugu

Which is pufferfish, a charming fish

That contains lethal quantities of a nerve agent, tetrodotoxin,

In its ovaries and liver. When I was a child, in 1998,

In a bad state with obsessive-compulsive disorder,

I carried the *Oxford Guide to Poisonous Animals*

With me everywhere I went. I'd feared

The smooth grey pufferfish and its neurotoxin for decades. Per annum

Between six and forty-eight people

Die from eating fugu. And here I was

Spending a lot of money to eat

Something I'd spent my life fearing would kill me

And that I didn't understand one bit.

The cultural significations of the dish, why the fish was treasured

Its subtle flavours – to my uneducated tongue, bland

And strangely cartilaginous – but the baths? And the beds?

Hey. A guy like me could get used to this.

I guess that's one way the system wins you over. Comfort.

But many of the things I loved

And turned to for comfort would end me if I let them.

Dopamine is the idiot god that lives in your brain that says,

More, I like *that*, *that* will fulfill me.

But even the dumbest of gods has things it can show you.

Dopamine offers great tutelage

That comes at a price. Dopamine teaches

How to chase pleasure

But chase pleasure too far it turns deadly.

Because the secret of pleasure –

The bathhouse orgy, the ryokan

The next hit, a sunset or sunrise

In a memorable place you paid to get to –

It's the things you profess to love the most

That most betray you eventually.

That voyage I went to Rabbit Island

Rabbits were my favourite animal for many years

We had a pet one, briefly

I couldn't pass up a trip to famous Rabbit Island

A former chemical munitions–testing base

Now overpopulated with leporine creatures

Escaped from the island's laboratory

You can take a train from Hiroshima

Then a ferry there, and bring carrots

Or lettuce, or whatever you can find,

Really, and meet thousands of rabbits.

The first hour I was on Rabbit Island

And rabbits ran up to me every ten metres

In groups of five to ten, fighting to

Nibble the carrots and alfalfa they are dependent

On tourists to bring them, I thought my heart would burst

From happiness, to see beautiful rabbits of many sizes, ages,

And colours. Surely this must be paradise on earth, if it exists.

But by the fifth hour and uncountable rabbit I was jaded. I was tired,

Dehydrated, I'd left early in the morning. I listened to a podcast

While I waited for the ferry to return. I'd grown

Resentful of the rabbits. Had to ration out

What food I'd brought them: there were so many

I'd have run out in minutes if I'd fed every bunny that I saw.

These rabbits were persistent and aggressive in their swarming;

The natural resources of the island were not set up to support them

And their success in multiplying without a predator nearby.

So they chase tourists as they spot them, knowing that

On them their dinner and survival both depend.

If you profess to love rabbits, do not seek Rabbit Island.

Rabbit Island shows you the lesson you've already learned

A thousand and one nights before this one:

The great secret of pleasure is that pleasure is empty.

But I too wanted to be perceived as a beautiful product

For a second I wanted to believe in the fantasy

That capitalism could be shinier

With a lower Gini coefficient and its faults obscured to me

By the idiot god that is touristry

That all of this around me wasn't spinning to the ground

In death throes lasting decades, or centuries

That the gambler knows, and the addict too

The truth that Dopamine is an envious god

He leads you to pleasure but he is a thief

And to him all pleasure is relinquished forever

The moment you hear him call out

In a voice that sounds quite like your own, *"Again."*

Restless in my bed that night I dreamed

Of pushing through translucent gelatine

Into another world

Everyone on earth imagines   But cannot yet see

Where this shit – Capital, in other words –

Didn't take so much

Brainpower, calories, energy

But now I have developed a taste for pufferfish

I do my rites for my idiot god

I put everything I own on black

On whether or not the next pleasure kills me

AT ANY MOMENT / WE CAN CHANGE

Solidarity nod to
Fellow gaijin I pass while out
Now I know what that's about
Now I know what that feels like
But I return to my "real life"
Jordan Peterson is in the news
He drifts into my brain
On an evil cloud I name Benzodiazepine
Jordan Jacob Petersonheimer Schmidt
His shame is my shame too
Whenever we go out
I missed the citrus blooms
But saw their fruits
The plum blossoms   But remain unimpressed
With a "free speech warrior"
Who amassed obscene wealth
And of all the drugs to get access to
Chooses common sedatives. Amateur.
But we each had   Our drugs of choice as well:
Snow melting into rain on the golden pavilion
The curve of the boys' asses at the public bath,
But not the boy I'm there with   Their thighs
A bad sleep a good fuck a Snorlax in bed
But reserving my inherent right
Of first refusal to a relapse on vacation
I poured the liquor in a vase behind my ear
Left the cigarettes in the toilet where I found them
Frenzied myself on coffee instead
Miserable   hot   sugary   beautiful   coffee
Canned from a vending machine
The substance whose withdrawals I have not engaged with since fourteen …
But far away   The other world

Moved onwards   Even in my sleep
My verdant dreams
Reeds protruding from a dried riverbank
Towering mountain of clouds   Gold leaf
An unreturned smile
Forcing a smooch upon his chapped lips
Floral upholstery   Dreams in cod French
A watchful crow named Jonathan
Before I sat on a Japanese toilet
Hadn't known I'd braced myself for cold for years
Why are we all still shitting on porcelain
Like Victorian orphans!
Stone slides carved into slate hills
Full moon over the Kamo River
Plum blossoms again. A breath of frost
Night fishing heron
Night fishing for bodies in its bony scaly claws
The tuft of hair hidden in his asscheeks
Sweat salt and the mysteries of an abdomen
An Ozzie of Aussies in blue formal wear
Drunk and spinning a whirligig globe
Here now always under
The sexy zenith of your powers
How the world has pulled me back in
All it took was a change of the backdrop
A little luxury
When I heard "Moves Like Jagger" in the airport
I knew I would always
Be alone   There at the end of my life
Back spasming   Dropping all the iron plates
Barbell slamming to the ground

THE YELLOW ROSE OF HIROSHIMA I

Meditating
Across from the A-bomb dome
Bent iron girders

I know about what happened. But today I am here to feel it

                                              Sadness isn't present

                              Why can't I make sadness be present?

But the sun is shining and I just had a good lunch and all these roses are in bloom

Guess I have no choice but to

Accept the conditions of the present as they are

Continue to pray for

A peace that will not come

THE WIND RELAPSING INTO

And there was no barrier to
Picking up a beer in "foreign" script
But my fear that the untravelled slope led
Off a cliff

And here there would be no
Real consequences. No one here knew me
The world would keep spinning
whether I had one drink
Or ten, sleeping through
The afternoon with a hangover
As familiar as my locale was exotic

My thought interrupted by
A cyclist nearly clipping me
There is no correct way to live

The only thing to change was
A choice made within a binary system
Just one choice after another
A single choice like the thousand and one
I'd made before this one, my
Finger on the coin slot in the vending machine
The trail of condensation
Running down the featureless, smooth glass

HIROSHIMA DOME UNDER NIGHT RAIN

It's Friday night in the public gym by the hypocentre's hollow

On a treadmill that charmingly displays

The various foods I work the caloric equivalent off on it

Banana follows sugar cube

I was putting one foot in front of the other

I was going for an aesthetic that said

I could kill you if I wanted to

Our savagery was Nature's doing

Vicious by nature

Sweetheart by choice

After choice after choice

THE YELLOW ROSE OF HIROSHIMA II

The events of the future *cannot* be inferred from those of the present.

– Ludwig Wittgenstein

What atrocities was I to get
The privilege of documenting for you?
Black rain
Canned Japanese coffee
As though to read a placard at the war museum
Was to   Live through this   To know
Stupid wounded child of peacetime

There's a toll to get in   My public tears
Two hundred millilitres   Their pain is my pain too
The melted Buddha statue that was underneath the blast
A child's dented lunch box   I see bloodstained clothing
I think of   smallpox blankets
Hey, God   What about us is worth saving?
An eco-fascist thought   Life tore a fear through me
But I, lucky, was to leave this place
And fuck somebody whose name I didn't know
If history were any indication

But history rhymed, never repeated

Today: it's peacetime
The sun falls peachy waves
On the standing walls
Of the A-bomb cathedral.

My mouth is full
Of Sachertorte

A yellow rose blooms in the peace pavilion garden
Six hundred metres from the hypocentre
Grand alleys   Gleaming trains
    Single-use disposable male masturbation product
Spring dares you to strip
Down to only what you need.
Today there is peace

        But the events of the future cannot be inferred from those of the present

MASSIVE ORDNANCE AIR BLAST II

In our merciless kingdom
divided by seven deltaic rivers
thriving with green frogs
details are being investigated.
The world ends with you

and also with you.

Blowing out the candles you wish
for rain to wash your body free
of all these unoriginal sins –

as if the weather ever
gave a shit what you wanted.

HOMONATIONAL ANTHEM

HOMONATIONAL ANTHEM

For Isabel Fall, and the victims of the 2022 Russo-Ukrainian war

Restrain also the keen fury of my heart
which provokes me to tread the ways of blood-curdling strife.
– *Homeric Hymn to Ares, trans. Hugh G. Evelyn-White*

Here the truceless armies yet
Trample, rolled in blood and sweat;
They kill and kill and never die;
And I think that each is I.
– *A.E. Housman*, A Shropshire Lad, *"The Welsh Marches"*

This is a poem
Composed of images
And words

Sometimes my words do not suffice

Here is a photo of Pete Buttigieg
Wearing cool guy wraparound shades
And camo fatigues
Holding a NATO M16 rifle
The sight of the rifle points down to the ground
He's standing in front of a lot of puppies
Dozens of them, various breeds

He posted the photo to Twitter
With the caption
"Time for 'therapy'!!!"

I remember September 11th.
And I remember the wars in Iraq and Afghanistan.
I remember how 2003 felt.
I remember My White Liberalism™.

My White Liberalism
Was easy. It was easy to
View the world
As consisting of good guys
And bad guys. I was a good guy
So were the politicians that were Not the Bad Guys.
Because we weren't the bad guys
If our military killed somebody
It must have been for the right reasons.
It really is that easy

You need to be a little sick
To walk around and evaluate the world
Through this kind of projective fantasy.

But a sick citizen
Is the most likely product
Of a sick nation in a sick society

And so I wrote this book.
About a different kind of fantasy

What if I could be the worst thing in the world
Which is to be both a faggot and arms dealer?

The book was out there,
There in the world.
Glittering like radon in the air
Like polyfluoroalkyl substance in my water

It was out there
It had been always out there
But now it had been made very apparent

Has it been made apparent to you in the intervening years?

Let me state here
Plainly
I am no enemy of any Ukrainian person.
What is happening to the people of Ukraine is unjust.
An injustice the likes of which I have not experienced.
A horror the likes of which I have not personally experienced.
A horror the likes of which I cannot yet personally understand.

But so were the wars in Iraq and Afghanistan

And so you'll excuse me when I say that
Though the conflict is unjust
As all armed conflicts are ultimately
As are all conflicts undertaken in the name of the nation-state

I remember the wars in Iraq and Afghanistan
I will not be fooled again

And I can tell
When you are trying to sell something to me

Here is a tweet by a news agency
It contains three rainbow flag emojis
It tells me about three handsome twinks
One ginger, one brunet, one blue-eyed
And how LGBTQ Ukrainians are fighting for their rights
By enlisting in the army

Oleg is a twenty-two-year-old bisexual man and beer sommelier!
Every day he wakes up
He shoots other twenty-two-year-old bisexual men in the skull
He takes a selfie just like I like to
The burlap strap that appends his machine gun to his body
Reads *please* in his native language.

Please.
Slay.

If you do, we might just view you as human.

Here's Saint Javelin

The Madonna

In a new, exciting role, redeemed

It has "become a popular symbol of the Ukrainian resistance"

The weapon she holds is a FGM-148 Javelin

Who manufactures this weapon?
Raytheon
And Lockheed Martin.

On February 18, 2022, a week prior to
"The special military operation"
The price of stock in Lockheed Martin
Was four hundred and fifty US dollars
Over the next week
You can watch the stock price climb
Up and to the right
The slope of it
Magnificent

I first encountered Saint Javelin
At the corner of Bay Street and Bloor Street
Where placards suggest
That NATO perform a decapitating strike
On the president of Russia
Read "no nuclear war in Toronto."
To this date, only two nuclear weapons have been used in the theatre of war
Both by a country that would become NATO
But facts share no daylight
With marketing

Of course it also depends
On what you consider the theatre of war to be

And to whom you extend the right of citizenry.

Were the bombs not dropped
On the indigenous peoples of the Marshall Islands?
Were the bombs not dropped on Bikini Atoll?
How about the Mescalero Apache in New Mexico?

And where did the uranium come from?

Did it come from the mines near Elliot Lake?

In the first decade of the 2000s, I was
A white child. I was a white child who grew up
In a town of the descendants of settlers,
Whose population was 71,446 persons
The year the twin towers "had fallen."
The year the twin towers had fallen.
A strange, passive construction.

The population of my home city
In the year the twin towers fell
Was 71,446, of which 2,290 persons
Were "of visible minority population,"
Which is about 3 percent.
Of which 390 residents
Self-identified as Black. Of which ninety-five
Residents self-identified as Arab.

I remember reading stories in the newspaper
About how nations in the Middle East
Hung people just for being gay.
How we didn't do that here.

                              And therefore our invasions were justified.

Some still run this line for Tel Aviv

There are some people who are, no doubt,
A threat to me and my liberty.
Perhaps even my right to
The safety and security of my body.
But I cannot discern
Who these people are
By looking at them.
I can infer they may be a threat to me
When I hear them speak of *perversion*
Or the *natural order* of society.
And where I live, those people are far more likely
To share with me a European ancestry

The place I feel the least safe
Will always be my home city

"Time for 'therapy'!!!"

I went home to my parents for dinner
In the year 2022
Where my grandfather rhapsodized
On how great it was to live in
My hometown when he was a kid,
Because the older guys he knew
Would chase anybody out they didn't recognize

And I nod along
Listening to the old man's story
Because I have only so many years of listening to his stories.
I don't share what I am thinking.

Which is: Who needed to be chased out of the city
Because the white residents thought
They didn't belong there?

You may correctly judge me a coward

I also remember
My grandmother's insistences
I never use the word *ain't*
She cared about the correctness of language
And so I became an adult who cared about language

So I now understand
What exactly it means to say
"Never say *ain't*"
To a white child

Another grandmother suggested I never say the word *hate*
A warning that time taught me to appreciate

But even the gesture toward myself as a child
And therefore innocent
Is part of the project of Whiteness
I cannot escape it

I remember in my home city
After the United States and Canada
"Secured" Afghanistan
And, crucially
Afghanistan's supply of opium poppy
A lot of kids in my white town died of an OD

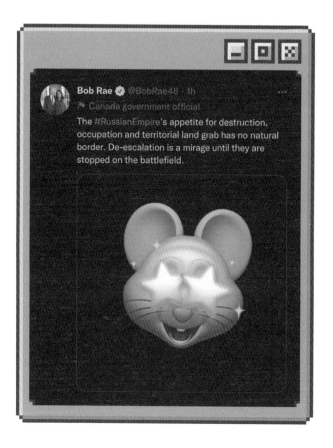

What appetites exactly does our empire deny itself?

Here is another image
Of a party on a cruise ship
I did not attend
The cruise's primary demographic
Is almost exclusively white wealthy gays
From major metropolitan areas in North America.
The men are shirtless and muscular
Almost exclusively.
These are aesthetic conditions to which
I aspire, if I'm honest, to fill some
Imagined inadequacy in myself.
Some of the men wear leather
Or Velcro harnesses with camouflage
Patterns as though of military issue.

Hundreds of gay men dancing
Everyone drunk or on drugs and shredded
Dressed like if we made armed combat
Look so fucking slutty, so sexy

What I find most disturbing
Is the balloons held by some of the men
Shaped like semi-automatic weapons.
You will note the distinctive shape
Of the AK-47, an automatic weapon
Designed for warfare
By Mikhail Kalashnikov
For the Soviet Union.

Here the Kalashnikov balloon
Serves as an emblem of
Masculinity, perhaps the
Testosteronic ideal of
Sex and aggression
Entwined or always close at hand,
Or perhaps just as a generic
Phallic or insertive symbol.

Here the distinctive shape
Is repurposed and removed from its
Original context as a weapon of
Slaughter, rape and misery
And placed in the context
Of a generic gay rave
Playing techno remixes
Of popular music with vocals
By Lady Gaga

One might note that
This weapon was once
A weapon of "the enemy"
Who threatened our "freedom"
And now I am to dance beneath it
As an emblem of my freedom

And here's another image, of a jockstrap manufacturer
Proud to launch their limited-edition Athletic Ukraine Classic Jockstrap
A shredded white model wears it
His toasted eight-pack foregrounded
By Ukraine's blue and gold

And now we are at war
Or is our empire's proxy

And as always
The people who make the decisions are not
The ones to suffer, and the image of the freedoms and rights of the common man
Are used to justify the slaughter of the same
Common men and women.
I only don't write "and nonbinary people"
In the line above
Because the metre is better

And I could point to images
Like the men dancing on this cruise ship
Or the twenty-two-year-old bisexual sommelier named Oleg
Or the limited-edition Athletic Ukraine Classic Jockstrap by Bike
If I wanted to say
That my name, image
Sympathy and likeness
Was being used to humanize the face of war
Irrespective of whether or not
Those wars were just or fair.
I do not personally believe
Any war is just or fair or necessary

But the world has always done very little
In the way of direct response
To my strongly held beliefs.

This place is not a place of honour

This place is not a place of honour

No highly esteemed deed is commemorated here

This place is a

Message ... and part of a system of messages ... pay attention to it!

Sending this message was important to us.
We considered ourselves to be a powerful culture.

Dulce et decorum non est.

The danger is still present, in your time, as it was in ours.

I criticize the use of images in this way
Yet one might say I am doing the same thing.
I too sought out the gay raves
Filled with shirtless men,
Not all wealthy and white, but mostly
For my art, for my fun,
My novel experiences, my dopamine
My community,
Maybe even my salvation

When I post a photo of my body
Do I reinforce the very bastions
I profess to want destroyed?

Here is another facet
Or image
Of my experience
Being a citizen of the world

Gay raves and the Internet
And war and immense suffering
Were all a part of the experience
Of being in the world
As I knew it.
Some of these things were
Immutable facts of the world

But not everything that was part of the world
Needed be part of the world forever

We needed to accept that
Many things were outside our control
If we wanted to feel happy
Ever again.

But yet I could not be resigned
To the inevitability of
Industrialized war
As an atomic fact of the world

I saw the Twitter feed of an artist I admire greatly.
She was a real radical in her heyday. Supportive,
Erudite and lovely. A lesbian
I saw her post about how Russians
As a people wanted this war
Because they were inherently
Despicable and bloodthirsty.
She posted on her Twitter page for everyone to see.
And in that moment I felt like I knew
Something I had known implicitly
From my studies of literature
That art was not
Inherently goodly

In fact, some artists could
And would use
Their powers to
Stoke the flames of war

I had read about this sort of thing before
In the poetry of Wilfred Owen
Who wrote his most famous poem
In response to a warmonger
Whose name we would have forgotten
If he hadn't written in response to her.
Her name was Jessie Pope.

Wilfred Owen loved Siegfried Sassoon.

My great-grandmother was a writer too.
My grandmother thinks I inherited that from her.
I've read her wartime love letters

This Christmas, my grandmother
Gave me a sketched portrait of
Siegfried Sassoon, drawn by
Seán O'Sullivan, who completed a portrait in
Oils of my grandmother when she was a child
That, as long as I've been visiting her house
Hangs above her mantelpiece.
This sketch of Siegfried Sassoon
Was part of my great-grandmother's estate
My grandmother passed it down to me.
It is part of my inheritance.

As is all the plunder and blood
It took for me to grow up
In the country we call Canada.

That is my inheritance too

Here I am like Siegfried Sassoon
Just trying to get my rocks off and write
Love poems to faggots and
Enjoy what's left of my waning beauty

Here I am feeling like Siegfried Sassoon
And I don't want to be
I did not think I would be.

I do not want to be feeling like Siegfried Sassoon
I had been told that we had ended history

I've quietly asked "the universe"
When I'm alone, late at night, to
For the sake of love
Make use of my body.

I've begged the universe
A little more loudly
To stop giving me material
For this genre of poetry

"For Raytheon Technologies, LGBTQIA+ inclusion means freedom to be yourself."

Lockheed Martin received a perfect score
On the Human Rights Campaign Foundation's
Corporate Equality Index for fourteen years in a row.

"I display my pictures [of my husband] to show anyone and everyone I am proud of who I am, and have never been more happy," said Raytheon subsidiary Pratt & Whitney manager Brian Kilhoffer.

"Bring your authentic self to a workplace that is diverse, equitable and inclusive."

I said there is no man
I could fuck in another world
That is my enemy in this one.

There is no man that is my enemy.
There is no man
Who can kill me.
To all men I give over
My heart and my body
And my power willingly

My freedom to fuck like this
Is contingent on the whims of the state
And could be revoked at any time.
So should I get down on my knees
And thank the state for the wars it wages
In the name of my sexual liberty.
Dulce et decorum est

Fuck you

I live in the time that I live in
The time that I live in is as cruel and unjust
As every other time has been before it

The circumstances into which I was born
Have favoured me for no reason other
Than that I was born into them
These things are immutable facts of the world

But between Siegfried Sassoon
My great-grandmother and me
Time shudders and collapses

Perhaps I am my great-grandmother
Reincarnated. Perhaps I've come here to
Learn the lessons that she failed to learn.

It is just one of many explanations for
Why at thirty I feel so fucking old
And tired, and more tired and old
Than my parents and grandparents
Seem to be, none of whom, while well-meaning
Seem to correctly perceive
The reality of the countries and societies they live in

But they lived in a different time

There will be many lessons that I fail to learn in life
I have made decisions future generations
Will correctly assess as short-sighted
Self-serving and cruel
I cannot say

Lockheed Changes Policy to Benefit Gays

By **Kirstin Downey**
November 23, 2002

Bethesda-based Lockheed Martin Corp., the nation's largest defense contractor, reversed course and added sexual orientation to its anti-discrimination policy, and said it plans to offer health benefits to the domestic partners of its gay employees.

The only thing that I know for sure
Is that somebody's making a killing.

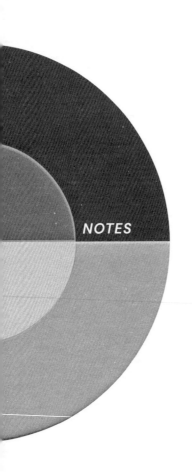

NOTES

NOTES, SOURCES, CITATIONS, INFLUENCES

"A BOUQUET OF KETCHUP-FLAVOURED ROSES"

"Here's a hundred / take me anywhere / just drive" paraphrases a line of dialogue from the 2007 film *Michael Clayton*.

The title is taken from a Canadian Valentine's Day promotion Frito-Lay ran in 2017, where contestants could enter a raffle to win a bouquet of "roses" fashioned from Doritos chips.

"You are caught in / a vast and inscrutable system / beyond your control" is a line from a painting by Canadian artist Noah Coyle.

"Panic grass and feverfew" is a chapter title from John Hersey's *Hiroshima* (1946).

"ADVENTURE TIME II"

Several concepts and terms in this poem are taken from Dungeons & Dragons, such as the concept of the lich, the word *cantrip* to refer to a low-level spell and the spell name Magic Missile.

"TAKE ME TO CHURCH"

"Take Me to Church" takes its title from the song by Hozier.

"In the race all runners run, but only one can win the prize" is adapted from 1 Corinthians 9:24, New International Reader's Version.

"BALLOONFEST '86"

"Balloonfest '86" recounts a poorly conceived promotional event run by the United Way of Greater Cleveland. Its epigraph is taken from the Wikipedia summary of the event.

"Drowning Ithacan sailor" is an unsubtle Eliot reference.

"Charity faileth not" is 1 Corinthians 13:8, King James Version.

"RAEKUURO"

I think *raekuuro* means *hailstorm* in Finnish, but I don't speak the language. Thanks to Piia for her lovely hospitality and tour of Old Helsinki.

"ANDERSON"

The concept of pigeons with backpacks being used as drug mules comes from *multiple* news reports on the subject in the mid-2010s, apparently to jails in Kuwait, Argentina, Costa Rica *and* Iran, which strains this author's credulity.

"THE HEART OF THE TOURIST IS EMPTY"

"I see the girls walk by dressed in their summer colds" is a mondegreen of the lyric from the Rolling Stones' "Paint It Black."

The eastern grotto referred to is the one at the Quinta da Regaleira in Sintra, Portugal. If you ever have the opportunity, you should go.

"My good bitch" was popular Internet slang in the mid-2010s.

"HAVING EXACTLY ALL OF IT"

This was originally written for *CV2*'s 2-Day Poem Contest in 2016 and was shortlisted for People's Choice prize. I have removed some of the words required for the contest.

"ADVENTURE TIME I"

"Adventure Time I," like "ATII," takes many concepts and ideas from popular fantasy.

"A flower that blooms / with the fragrance of mischief" is adapted from "flavour text" on the Magic: The Gathering card titled Bitterblossom. All rights reserved Hasbro.

"Shadow Word: Pain" is the title of a spell from *World of Warcraft.*

"Gemsteel" is a fictional material from the *Final Fantasy* series of video games. "Irukandji stingers" refer to the Irukandji jellyfish, which is *not* fictional.

"Easy Mac" refers to the old brand name for the Kraft processed macaroni product now titled Macaroni and Cheese Dinner cups.

"Undiscovered country" is *Hamlet*.

"AFTER EIGHT"

Takes its title from the Nestle-owned candy.

The drunk man kicking an otter to death in the street is something my friend Ali Pinkney actually witnessed, and is recounted in her novella *Roadkill Croque Monsieur.*

Although there are no direct or indirect references, I was reading Ben Lerner's *The Lichtenberg Figures* directly prior to this poem's composition.

"KELETI STATION"

The incident referred to in this poem is the firing of reporter Petra László for being caught on video kicking immigrants as they crossed the Hungarian border, and the subsequent media firestorm that attracted international attention and comment, including from Hungarian autocrat Viktor Orbán.
 The incident is now largely forgotten.
 Orbán claimed, as all autocrats do, that Hungary's culture needed "defending" from immigrants.

Lángos is a *cultured* flatbread usually deep-fried, not unlike a savoury version of Canadian mass-market treat BeaverTails.

Fény is a brand name belonging to Zwack, the Hungarian spirits company, however, it is used as a generic trademark for any pálinka that has been carbonated.

The poem incorporates the names of several popular Budapest tourist destinations, landmarks or main thoroughfares.

The line "Under a sky expressionless and cold as a denied visa" is actually a bit of self-plagiarism. I originally wrote it in a poem in 2009 or 2010 titled "Lampedusa," about the tragedy of Libyan immigrants drowning when attempting to cross the Mediterranean Sea into Italy. From 2010 to 2017, between five hundred and five thousand people seeking refugee status in Europe drowned in the Mediterranean Sea *annually.* "Lampedusa" will never be published, but its best line lives on.

"KREUZBERG"

"Retractable claws" is one of the "powers" of Wolverine, one of the fictional X-Men. (Actually, his power is the ability to heal from nearly any wound, which allowed him to survive the operation that grafted the adamantium onto his bones.)

"Manufacturers come and go / talking of debt-to-earnings ratio" is Eliot again. Eliot's music will always play inside my brain, but I now view him more as an ancient enemy whom I begrudgingly respect than a figure to look up to.

"Lampedusan blood gelée" – see the notes for "Keleti Station."

"Absolute dud" is a nuclear weapon that fails to undergo its fission (or fusion) reaction.

This poem's final stanza rewrites, or interpolates, the final verse on Kanye West's 2012 single "Mercy," written and performed by American rapper 2 Chainz. Since last edit, Kanye's rhetoric got a lot more Hitler-y and I gotta put it out there – it's too late for me to rewrite this part but I don't condone a single fucking thing Kanye believes.

"EQUINOX"

The story the grandmother figure tells is a loose synopsis of a plot from one of the Classical Kids books-on-tape that my grandparents played for us in the car sometime in the final years of the twentieth century. I did not feel like purchasing the collection to find out which.

"[ASSETS NOW IN PLAY]"

Carthage is Virgil, obviously.

The iPad funerals alluded to at the end of the poem were a cultural phenomenon that occurred during the earliest stages of the ongoing SARS-CoV-2 pandemic.

"HALL OF A HUNDRED REFLECTIVE SURFACES"

The boy attempting to spell *anodyne* with chunks of ice is from Hans Christian Andersen's "The Snow Queen." Kay has been bewitched by a cursed mirror invented by one of Satan's lesser attendants. The Snow Queen captured him, but promised him liberation if he could spell the word *eternity* out of ice.

"My fingers in his wound" is a reference to depictions of Thomas the Apostle.

"WASTED"

Someone else gave me the number of calories a sun salutation expels. If you are reading this and recognize yourself, I hope you are well, I miss you and I'm very sorry for stealing a detail from your life.

"KISS FROM A ROSE"

The title refers to the 1994 song by Seal.

"PROTECTIVE WEIRDING"

Storm glass is used incorrectly here – it is not a material, but a device. Here I flash my poetic licence.

Twenty-sided die and "fortitude save against charisma" are both Dungeons & Dragons again.

"BOTTLED"

We have Robert Frost and Peggy Lee in here.

"HEIR CONSUMPTIVE"

"Give me Librium, or give me meth" is *The Boys in the Band*.

"HOW SHOULD A PERSON BE?"

This title belongs to Sheila Heti's book by the same name.

"CLOUD OF UNKNOWING"

This poem depicts the 2017 Grenfell Tower fire in London.

Archimedes did not use mirrors to burn ships, but it is commonly held that he did.

"THE SUN HAS NEVER LOOKED SO LARGE"

More self-plagiarism, which I prefer to call a motif: I'm riffing on my own line "high horse chestnut spanning aeons," which is from "LONG POEM II," not in this collection.

"MASSIVE ORDNANCE AIR BLAST I"

The poem takes its title from the official name of the GBU-43/B Massive Ordnance Air Blast or MOAB, also known as the "mother of all bombs," which, when it was dropped on Afghanistan in 2017, was the largest conventional (i.e., non-nuclear) explosive weapon ever used.

"No human language can withstand the speed of light" is Baudrillard, from *The Illusion of the End*.

"HOW PERILOUS IS PURITY OF HEART"

"Blue roses" is both David Lynch and Tennessee Williams.

"FOUR-MINUTE WARNING"

A lot of ambient "Russiagate" paranoia in this one, including the "deep state" lines.

"I am not an atomic playboy" was a line issued in a press statement by US vice-admiral William Blandy, who oversaw the Operation Crossroads atomic weapons tests in Bikini Atoll.

The Bikini Atoll islands belong to the Marshallese people. They were forcibly relocated in 1946 so the US and their allies could test nuclear weapons. The Bikini Atoll is still today too radioactive to safely support human life.

As "reparations" for this violent act, the US established a trust fund for the families who were relocated. The fund contains more than $82 million and pays out less than $15,000 annually to each beneficiary.

"Hellfire enters the hospital" refers to the 2015 Kunduz Trauma Centre hospital airstrike in Afghanistan by the US Air Force. At least thirty people were killed, many of them civilians.

"THE BOMB IS THE BUDDHA OF THE WEST"

This poem's title is taken from *The Illusion of the End* by Jean Baudrillard.

"You could call it the mother of all coalitions" quotes Donald Rumsfeld, referring to the Multi-National Force – Iraq coalition that invaded Iraq. Canada has never formally admitted to its participation in the coalition. Details of Canada's participation are known to Canadian government officials, but were never shared with Parliament or the public.

The Castle Bravo test was one of the Bikini Atoll weapons tests.

The "forty-two children are murdered" figure conflates the Biblical story of Elisha (2 Kings 2:20) and reports of the number of civilians killed in the 2017 al-Jinah mosque airstrike by the United States Armed Forces.

I do not have a primary source for the Ko Un anecdote, but it has been widely reported on.

The last two lines allude to Ko Un's "Ear," translated by Suji Kwock Kim and Sunja Kim Kwock, originally published in *Poetry*.

"'Cuz *bomb*'s such an old-fashioned word" is a riff on the final bridge of "Under Pressure" by Queen and David Bowie.

"ON THE THIRTY-NINTH DAY OF RAIN"

Title is Genesis. The bible, not the band.

"On Wednesdays, we wear [X]" is *Mean Girls*.

"God took me / so many places already ... I just want to stay where I am" quotes Harry Dean Stanton's character from David Lynch's *Twin Peaks: Fire Walk with Me*.

"My matte bronze powders" is from Twitter novelty account Kim Kierkegaardashian (@KimKierkegaard).

"WINDOWS XP FOR OHIO-CLASS SUBMARINES"

This poem's title refers to multiple news reports circulating in 2016 that Britain's Trident nuclear submarines used Windows XP as their operating system. The UK Ministry of Defence has since disputed this claim.

"The fattening silence of bombs" is a riff on Mary Ruefle's "the calorific sadness of bombs."

"TRANS-PACIFIC"

"A sight to stopper ancient women's hearts" is me riffing on Ariana Reines riffing on Eliot's "ancient women / gathering fuel in vacant lots."

"These truths appeared to me self-evident" is the US Declaration of Independence.

"Getting more / of our valuable natural resources to global markets" would have been taken from some ad I'd encountered on the plane when I wrote this. Probably oil or mining, maybe HSBC.

"TO THE GENERATIVE POWER OF THE"

"Acidulated roses" is almost certainly from perfume writers Luca Turin or Tania Sanchez, although I don't have a quote.

"POEM FOR KEN"

"Hunger is the choicest seasoning" is a riff on the proverb "hunger makes the best sauce."

"EN ROUTE TO ZOSHIGAYA STATION"

"Cosmetics for foreigners" is found text from an ad I saw in Tokyo somewhere.

"KEN"

The time eating metaphor (including stomach) is inspired by Keith Douglas's "Time Eating," which I had not read for about fifteen years prior to writing this.

More Eliot here.

"INFINITE CRYSTAL UNIVERSE"

Infinite Crystal Universe is an interactive sculpture by teamLab at their teamLab Planets attraction in Toyosu, Tokyo.

"Captive Apple" is the URL protocol launched when joining a public Wi-Fi network via an iOS device.

"KYOTO"

"The heart of the tourist is empty" is, although it feels silly to have to note it, from the poem of the same name earlier in this book.

"A TASTE FOR PUFFERFISH"

The book I refer to is actually *Amazing Poisonous Animals* in the Eyewitness book series, authored by Alexandra Parsons and published by Alfred A. Knopf Books for Young Readers in 1990.

"AT ANY MOMENT / WE CAN CHANGE"

Snorlax is property of the Pokémon franchise owned by Nintendo/Creatures Inc./ Game Freak Inc.

"THE YELLOW ROSE OF HIROSHIMA I"

The "yellow rose" of the title is actually the unofficial nickname for the town of Amarillo, Texas – "The Yellow Rose of Texas" – where many nuclear weapons are assembled. I would have encountered this information when conducting research at the Banff Centre for Arts and Creativity's library in 2017. I was thus delighted to discover yellow roses in bloom at the Hiroshima Peace Memorial Park three years later.

"THE WIND RELAPSING INTO"

I think "There is no correct way to live" is something my therapist said to me once, but I'm not sure.

"THE YELLOW ROSE OF HIROSHIMA II"

Thanks to Ariana Reines for her editorial advice on an earlier draft of this poem.

"Black rain" refers to the contaminated rain that fell over Hiroshima and Nagasaki after the United States dropped nuclear weapons on them. It contained a lot of combusted material and nuclear fallout. It sickened and killed tens of thousands.

The Wittgenstein epigraph is from the *Tractatus*.

"MASSIVE ORDNANCE AIR BLAST II"

"Seven deltaic rivers" and "details are being investigated" are, as above, from John Hersey's *Hiroshima*.

"The world ends with you / and also with you" juxtaposes the name of a Square Enix video game released in 2007 and the common Roman Catholic mass refrain.

"HOMONATIONAL ANTHEM"

Various images from Twitter.

"This place is not a place of honour" is Internet copypasta, attributed to Twitter user Steve Lieber by Know Your Meme, now widely disseminated, with text from white paper "Expert Judgment on Markers to Deter Inadvertent Human Intrusion into the Waste Isolation Pilot Plant," written by Kathleen M. Trauth, Stephen C. Hora and Robert V. Guzowski, commissioned by Sandia National Laboratories, Albuquerque, NM, for the US Department of Energy.

Sandia National Laboratories are owned by Honeywell International Inc. and are part of the US/NATO's nuclear weapons and research programs in New Mexico.

Text on page 145 is lifted from public corporate communications on "diversity initiatives" by Raytheon and Lockheed Martin, www.rtx.com/news/2022/05/17/for-raytheon-technologies-lgbtqia-inclusion-means-freedom-to-be-yourself.

The image on page 150 is from the *Washington Post*.

While not directly referenced due to changes made during the process of editing and composition, *Celebrate Pride with Lockheed Martin* owes a special intellectual debt to the following texts:

Orientalism by Edward W. Said
Terrorist Assemblages: Homonationalism in Queer Times by Jasbir K. Puar
The collected works of Frederick Seidel
Look by Solmaz Sharif
Psychological Aspects of Nuclear War by James Thompson
100 Suns by Michael Light
At Work in the Fields of the Bomb by Robert Del Tredici

ACKNOWLEDGEMENTS

ACKNOWLEDGEMENTS

To my partners, Graeme and David, and my little cat!

To Ken Tanaka.

To my family. Please buy but do not read this book!

To David Bradford and Domenica Martinello for their manuscript consultations on the earliest draft of this book, and encouraging me to not toss it.

To Karen Solie and Ocean Vuong for their guidance at Banff in 2017.

To the Montreal Poetry Group for earlier editorial help, and to the Blue Chip Poets: Rose, Dan, Helette and Allison.

To all my creative writing instructors over the years for their invaluable advice and encouragement: Sue Goyette, Melanie Little, Sina Queyras, Kate Sterns and Bill Clarke.

To everyone at Wolsak & Wynn for being patient and gentle with me.

To Liz Howard for her generous reading and helping me uncover what book this book wanted to be. Prior to her involvement, I did not want to publish this.

To Ariana Reines for her editorial advice, and her poetics.

To Jackson Teather.

To friends Noah Coyle, Adèle Barclay, Cassidy MacFadzean, Liam Lachance, Scott Cecchin, Dare Williams, Ali Pinkney, Domenica Martinello, Marcela Huerta, James Chapman, Vicki Donkin, Kyle Flemmer, Kirby, Andrea

Bridgman, Melanie Power, Eli Tareq el Bechelany-Lynch, Tarik Dobbs, Dina del Bucchia, Ayman Itani, Kysan Kwan, David Demchuk, Alex Manley, Tara McGowan-Ross, Joni Murphy, Joshua Wales, Jen Sookfong Lee, the members of Invisible College. Also to my friends who are not artists, who keep me sane.

To the Canada Council for the Arts and the Conseil des Arts et des Lettres du Québec for their material support, and to the Toronto Reference Library.

JAKE BYRNE is a poet and writer based in Toronto, Canada. Their work has been published in journals and anthologies in North America. Their poem "Parallel Volumes" won *CV2*'s Foster Poetry Prize for 2019, and their first two books of poetry are forthcoming in 2023 with Wolsak & Wynn and in 2024 with Brick Books, respectively. Find them @jakebyrnewrites.